White Ghosts

White Ghosts

Katie Hale

Nine
Arches
Press

White Ghosts
Katie Hale

ISBN: 978-1-913437-66-4
eISBN: 978-1-913437-67-1

First published March 2023 by:

Nine Arches Press
Unit 14, Sir Frank Whittle Business Centre,
Great Central Way, Rugby.
CV21 3XH
United Kingdom

www.ninearchespress.com

Printed in the United Kingdom by Imprint Digital on recycled paper.

Nine Arches Press is supported using public funding
by Arts Council England.

Supported using public funding by
**ARTS COUNCIL
ENGLAND**

for Val, Dot, Katie, Lucy, Mary,
Elizabeth, Peggy, Jane, Lucy, Mary & Mary

and for the women whose names
were never written down

Contents

Census, 1810

in those days only white men
were born with names

tallied   *free white persons*   *females*

/

tallied   *number of slaves*

/

each stroke wide enough to hide a life /
each a rifle barrel aiming at a voice /

each a match lit to exhaustion /
a cavity / rough rot in the tooth

filling the mouth with bad taste
with the tongue of omission /

Genesis (1)

And so the first woman went out from the continent of her birth, and occupied the land of Virginia, on the east of the Americas.

And the woman knew her husband; and she conceived, and bare a daughter, who bare a daughter, who builded a plantation.

And unto this plantation was born Mary; and Mary begat Mary, and Mary was the mother of Lucy.

And they called the name of this plantation, after the name of their great desire, Home.

Portrait of My Great Great Great Great Great Great Great Grandmother as Emily Shelby in *Uncle Tom's Cabin*

'a bitter, bitter, most accursed thing! – a curse to the master, and a curse to the slave!'

a white woman stands at the casement
demanding, *and is there nothing to be done?*

her back to the window, shuttered shut –
with braided hair, in her blue silk gown,
her rope of pearls, their prized white grit – again
she asks her husband, is there nothing to be done?

hers is an ensemble story. the house girl
slips a warming pan between the cotton.
some days, the sheets are sails. some days
a shroud, and there is nothing to be done

but let her husband slip between her body,
between the body of the house girl he owns
the way he owns the casement, pearls,
the blue silk gown. so nothing to be done

but let her own white body bulge, a hogshead
of leaf, a coin-fat purse, a slow stone
pearling in her belly. already she is passing on
the blood-lie: there is nothing to be done.

through her blue silk breast, through the milk
of a wet-nurse (her own child gone),
through umbilical blood: this is how the pearl
will learn to witness, learn the nothing-to-be-done.

and so the white woman teaches the house girl
her letters. each word is a gift, she says – a ribbon
glossy with its own white creed – a knotted
blood-cord at the base of both their tongues.

'let your mouth give birth to the words, to the body
of text. read with me: *and. is. there. nothing. to. be. done.*'

*

a white woman stands at the casement
demanding

        the window shuttered shut
    braided hair   her blue silk gown
her rope of pearls   prized white
          husband

                the house girl
    warming
      the sheets

           the house girl
      owns
             nothing

     her own   body

     belly

                       milk

and so the white woman
           says –

let your mouth give
      me   *nothing*

*

a white woman

                                is   nothing

her   story

a shroud

        her husband

                owns the casement, pearls,
the blue silk gown

                her own white body
                        fat   slow
                                already   he is passing on

                her blue silk breast

                to witness

                                        the house girl

glossy with
                        both their tongues.

'let   the words,   the body
                                        be done.'

*

and is there nothing

                                to be done?

let
    the body

learn to witness

   its own white
               tongue

*

a white woman stands at the casement
demanding

a   story

her own   body

her own

witness

own

words

*

white woman
demanding

her

      own   casement

her own
coin-fat purse

her own

house girl

*

the house girl

sails some days

between her body,
the body of
the casement,

the   lie

of   her own child

the house girl
says
no

give birth to
nothing

Study of the Slaver as a Door

the one at the bottom of the garden where we played   ivy-bound   obstinate
   whiteness flaking   the adults barbecued with their backs to it
and said   *children, come away*   on the other side   nothing we
wanted much   the wall was loose with brick-holes   we had all seen
the meadow   yellow rapeseed in spring   summer die-back when earth
bared its stomach   insects buried themselves to survive   and on
the cusp of winter when rains came and the door swelled shut against the
flood   we'd see the bones emerge   sprout from soil in rings   biscuit-
brittle   round   mushrooming bodies   brought back to their minimal
parts   because we knew even then   water can make the toughest
of us give up our secrets   once there was a woman in our family
   wore the key to this crumbling door around her scented neck   let her
fingers drift there sometimes as she opened a window   ran them across it
      a lock of lover's hair   but she's gone now   and where the
key is nobody can tell   though they say the woman took it   skeletal
and small   to her six-foot plot on the hill

DOORS OPEN
INWARD

Sign at the entrance to Christ Church, Lancaster County, Virginia, where the
first recorded women in my family are buried

Prayers

We believed in progress
but the law was against us.

It was difficult
for us, this caged existence.

Sundays, we slogged the two rough miles
to the church on the hill,

donned good shoes to pray
for emancipation. Up in the gallery

our enslaved prayed along.
There were no stairs, and the door

was shut to them, so they climbed
a ladder to the window.

And when the preacher said *equals*
we shouted *equals.*

And when he said *brethren*
we shouted *brethren.*

And when he called for abolition
our affirmations burst

in zealous flocks
to flutter at the timbered ceiling.

And we were spectacular
in our radicalism. Our fervour

flayed the chords from our throats.
It rattled the bottle glass panes.

And the next week we returned,
and we beseeched the almighty again.

Inheritance

i.

Listen. It was a time when the sea
laid herself down as a cape on the road,
bade the women in my family cross
keeping their boots dry –

                    though they spoke
with the voices of hawks, their words
cunning, ungilt, and the menfolk
never laid a thing at their feet –

women who sweated
with weight muscled forward,
kneading the ground, their hands
rough birds alighted on a broken fence,
braced for the snarl of dogs.

They bore in the soft of their gut
the barbed journey west,
their husbands' whiskey breath,

and they were not me
and I am not them, but still
look upon these women
who owned slaves.

ii.

Let yourself picture a shuttered house,
chinks of light at the clapboard
and a bricked-up chimney,

ring-marked pigeon with a broken wing.
It flaps and claws – the sound
is almost the sound of words:

muffle of dirt
once a chequered tablecloth
laden with dishes, a feast

but there is no food in the house
and I think I might be the pigeon –
though perhaps

I might be the house,
choir of wood and bent nails
groaning, unsettling the dust.

iii.

quivering years she waited in the dark   dormant at the heart of
the house   /   she herself was not the house   but the old log
cabin inside the house   /   prairie dwelling   rough-wood sides
plastered over   whole and hearth   closed fist   memory borne
in the gut   /   generations later   the men came   accidentally
scalpelled her loose   /   bare and unguarded   she smarted in
the dust-blade air   an excavated frontier   /   timber by timber
they unlocked her   bore her off   resettled her in the belly of
the town's museum   /   for five dollars a day   you can see her
   commit your ghosts to her still

iv.

In the town's one museum, between the wall of guns and the reconstructed log house, is a wooden board, pinned with cuts of wire. The interpretation label explains how barbed wire enabled segmentation of the flatlands and penning of cattle. This revolutionised ranch farming, and ultimately facilitated land ownership across the United States.

Meanwhile, the women in my family braced their bodies
against the dawn. Meanwhile, they stood at the door,
mist feathering the prairie,
sky the colour of afterbirth. Meanwhile

barbed seeds were spawning.

flat ribbon / Glidden / Brinkerhoff / double barb

Come spring, wire sprouted
from difficult soil, grew tall as switchgrass,
metal fronds that tapped and tangled in wind

until they blossomed, and at the height of a man
bore fruit: ripe coils
the enslaved folk had to pluck

till their fingers shone
with metal dust, their thumbs stung.

Kelly / reverse twist / Ellwood / single strand

Even the women of the household
ate the fruit – gorged till their chins ran mercury.

You cannot rescue them, nor any of my family.

Washburn / Haish / Crandal / diamond point

v.

The wind hisses in my great great grandmother's voice –

All those godfearing years I let prairie-dust
score at my face, the bastard sun blister
my scalp, bugs scratch a living at my seams –

muddied my hands to the elbow in our stark
allotted soil, and all to give my daughters
a crop worth the reaping. All so their skin

in the shadows of neat-hemmed skirts
remained adored – unsullied – white.
Guard it, child – your smuggler's hoard.

vi.

So I slip
ghostlike
between the narrow wharfs

of my people,
women ghost
the unlit galleys of my veins,

my skin mutters
like sea ice, ghostdom
in the sunless winter, and I

am a ship in the cracks.
I follow the creaks,
the saltwater leads

to where they freeze, knit
themselves shut.
Find myself

winter-bound, miles from anywhere.

Genesis (2)

And so Lucy begat Jane; and also a son, who called up the name of his country; and he led into battle the husband of his sister, and many other men alongside.

And after, took unto himself a wife, Priscilla; and a community of slaves, who did bury him with her, in a tomb on his own land.

The Priscilla (1830s)

for Jane, my great great great great great great grandmother

Some days the ghosts forget they don't belong,
push through like tough buds
spat from the mouths of trees.

Some days they drip from branches in the first sun,
a collapsing constellation
leasing the sky from its bond.

We cannot navigate by ghosts, though we are still,
so many of us, trying.

*

Somewhere in Kentucky, your brother
constructs another boat: his annual devotion
of sawing, chiselling, hollowing out,
the peeling of bark from the pulp.

Each year, he says he's building up to hunting.
Each year, you know he is missing his wife.

For weeks he sheds his blue velvet coat
at the back of the plantation, queued hair
a frisson of wood dust, a rare ritual: perspiring
his own sweat, setting his own muscles to task.

Each day heaps rags like an offertory,
anoints his hands with linseed. Each night
he washes them from the jug in the pitch-dark house.

He says he does this to honour his wife.
You know he does it for himself.

*

Sometimes, don't you also lose yourself
in the making of things: dip and release

of needle, veins of thread
beating with your own small loss?

Some days, your husband smokes. Others
he says the food turns to ash in his mouth.

When he wakes from dreams of the Regiment,
you hold him as you held your small daughter,

just once. Lean into his grieving, let it absorb you
like splattered oil in the dust.

*

Some days you picture your brother
and his latest Priscilla:
completed for the summer on the creek,

new prow nosing the bank, his fishing line
waking such depths. This is your brother's
own pursuit of happiness:

catching wild turkey in his sights;
the fan and fall of their military
red coats. We all have our personal ghosts.

*

Some say to purge a house of grief,
burn bundles of sage bound with black ribbon,

employ a priest
to say a prayer beyond the threshold.

This will cause a restless spirit
to move on. In the lane

behind the cotton fields, one narrow tree
still clings for all it's worth

to last year's habits, and all the curt bay winds
cannot persuade them loose.

*

Somewhere in your brother's barn, all his wifeless years
are stacked like hollow bones, their single summers spent.

Somewhere, your brother has hung
barn doors across his chest, has nailed them shut.

And somewhere in the heartlands, something
is building, oarless as a heap of linseed rags.

Inevitable, waiting for the moment to combust.

Song

In the beer-stocked basements of clapboard bars,
      in the concrete pipe that passes
         beneath the freeway, in the dregs
            of dirt that settle the base of it
         smelling of summers
                drifted here to die,

is where the women in my family wait:
my great grandmother and all her mothers

      whispering their ghost gossip in words
the living cannot understand.
              There are cliques among the dead, too –
      and they have their own terms
            for colours,
        for pale roots of corn, the khaki grit of a bypass,
        for the reptilian cross-hatchings of skin.

When the world perches
         on the brink of rain,
        sometimes you can hear them
         singing,

      sounding their words through the woodwind night

      so for a moment
         a tune might come to you
            unbidden,
and the wind in the cottonwoods is almost
              a familiar face.

Talking With My Great Great Great Great Great Great Grandmother at a Fast Food Diner off the Interstate in Virginia

She orders fries, a supersize Mountain Dew. Delighted, belches at the bubbles. Orders waffles. She squirts on mustard, then mayonnaise, then ranch. She sees me looking. Shrugs.

You miss the flavours, being dead.

Her chin is slick with meat-grease from a quarter pounder. In the strip-light above the window, she gleams, more ghost than body. I can see my own reflection through her.

My grandfather, he held land in France
and the title *Marquis*
and later, as a Huguenot, he lost it.

Sure, we knew our rank, our value, our class –
but we understood *home* by what was torn away from us.

Girl, don't think we had it easy.

As a child, I learned
the ritual cinching of waists,
washing my face before dawn,
learning to keep my pale skin
from the sun.

I taught my daughters
how to dance a minuet in the French style,
the rise and fall, how to follow
a man's direction, to move without substance or weight.

Outside is just the road, a string of lights, a passing on –

Back then we called them *fancy dances,*
and this was how they set themselves apart
from other girls, who only knew the jigs and common reels –

the farming girls,
the beggar girls,
the slaves.

Reaching for biscuits, she mops her gravy, cuts swathes across the plate.

The slaves were in my husband's name – not mine.

The whole place reeks of fat, regret, and day-old coffee.

You know my husband fought the revolution?
Monmouth
Germantown
Brandywine Creek –

at each your British forces
spat towards him, bloody teeth
with gunshot bites, and the living
backed up in the ravine to die like fish
half in, half out of the river –
and all for the ideal of *America.*

People like us, we built this country
from nothing, from the dust.

A victory of half-drunk soda, empty dishes. Neon tubing flickers like
lightning. She gathers leftovers closer in like clouds.

My brother, also, was a soldier
and a personal friend of Lafayette.

You know, when the French general returned
years later, it was my brother's daughter
scattered flowers in his path,
and Lafayette, the gentleman he was,
refused to walk on them –

wouldn't crush the petals, he said,
that had been laid with such devotion.

Can you imagine?

For a man of battle – such kindness,
such concern for the labour of others?

A 17th Century Guide to Beauty in Virginia

Come,
in the owl-time, in the shy fox-hour, coyotes

still courting the moon, silver creek
of the Milky Way glinting

above the Rappahannock River
in a fist of flung shillings –

come, dip your face
to the dew, each drop its own

loose change, waiting
to be slipped into the charity box of dawn.

Spend them liberally, soaking your cheeks
in the tears of your not-yet-country –

till with a stirring of snuff-dark breath
the shuttered eyes of the household

blink awake, and the sun begins again
its daily scouring of soil beneath tobacco leaves.

All day the plants will stake their hard
aromas to your brow, your unwashed palms.

All day you will catch your tongue
lamenting, reimbursing their murmured aubade.

And in the sequel

the sisters reconciled, the kingdom thawed,
the comic snowman rescued from the melt,
we follow a voice towards the northern people –

to where the king once dammed the water,
where he tried to massacre the villagers,
where he named his interference *gift*.

Go back far enough, a story always tells itself –

like the time, digitising the collection
of lichen for New York's Botanical Gardens,
you exhumed from the archives of the herbarium

a matchless silver mountain range,
blood sun bursting from a saffron cloud:

'*caloplaca elegans* – collected: Fort Chimo, Canada'
also: '*physcia ciliata* – on bone of Eskimo child'

[we apologise: artefacts in the cabinet of First Peoples
have been removed for conservation]

The Gallery of America

The streets were paved with gum and flung cigarettes
and I needed to get out of the rain.

The promised rains were not falling. The heat in the city
was velvet, the gallery pale and kept conditioned.

The gallery was warm, and westerlies whetted
and cut to the quick. I presented my ticket at the desk

and the unsmiling man let me in. The bulbs were old-school
and golden, wistful as honey in winter, the walls

cluttered with the burnished and gilt.
And there was ugliness in the gallery, but the audioguide

manoeuvred me away. The stairwell flickered
and was difficult to climb. From the thresholds

invigilators orbited like drones. Still, I was told
I belonged in the gallery

though I was a curiosity and uncurated.
I trod mud on the marble but nobody asked me to leave.

Later, I was reading Rankine in the gallery café
where all the servers were black and the white punters

pretended not to notice, where none of us
paid our tabs, or offered to take our receipts,

where our mounting waste subsumed the bussing station.
This may have been part of the exhibition.

Genesis (3)

And Jane begat Peggy, who with her husband Heritage did cross the great forest to the west; and Peggy begat Elizabeth.

And Heritage did lay claim to rich earth; and to four slaves, whose names are known only to the lord; one who was female, of adult years; and three boys who were not yet grown.

Ghosts

            Tonight, they are a skulk
        of foxes circling the bed

                footfalls
soft
            as dropped gloves

                eyes
        constellations in the dark –

but there is no alpha star,
no matriarch.
                In the tail-light
they ripple their superb fur,
            fox-fire
phosphorescent on the carpet.
            From their muzzles
    comes a smell of scrag
                foul
                birth-matter of lambs.

            One day, will I go with them –
        will I take fox-form –

            city fox,
            fox of the farm and the scattergun hens,
sister to the litter or vixen aunt –

learn to choose
                between righteousness
            and the fox?

Will I gather
in the dreams of my daughters
saying,

     Come
          skulk –

     come, let us scavenge –
          come

               let us be plunderers
               of carrion, of ripe meat?

daughter

after Warsan Shire

your eyes are shod hooves on a thoroughfare
lungs twin boulders   a recipe for thunder
your mouth a border quartering the dirt
from hunger

                    your first thoughts
how the air is made for wailing through
your tinder heart for blazing through

your feathered tongue already soaring
away   away across the water

Peggy and Her Husband Heritage
Cross the Monongahela Forest, 1800s

Beaver dams harvest the creeks.
A blood spray of robins shivers
blossom from black cherry trees.

At the lip of a paddock
is a chained horse. Her foal
purples in the long grass.

A turkey vulture lumbers into flight
as you hie the intestinal turnpikes,
wend up like a copperhead

searching for a muscle of soil
to spike. You decorate your hood
with the cloud bank's delicate beads,

each drop a nation
fractured in a seed of light.

Heritage Lays Claim to One Hundred and Sixty Acres of Unfarmed Land in Missouri

for Peggy, my great great great great great grandmother

At night his body was a meadow and she
was an unbridled horse
bending at a still pool to drink.

She lay down in him
and wept, because smiling
was not enough

and he covered her like tall grasses,
an abundance. She was lost
at the heart of him

and whole, his breath
a warm breeze
carrying summer to her skin, tender

as a child
might bring to the house
an armful of wildflowers.

His touch was an exquisite storm
and he tore through her like fire –
birds and deer mice fleeing

till there was only smouldering
calm. Then slowly
emergence

of chicory, of henbit.
Slowly her mouth
was yarrow, budded healing.

She kissed the rich earth of his chest,
scent of wandering rains, covered him
like a paling dome. At dawn, rose

a swooping chorus of orioles, a feathered
gift. He offered them to her
plattered – crackle of exquisite bones.

Ternary

i.

My mother's song was a caterpillar
trundling a city of grass,

was grass
giving in to the wind –

it scoffed on light, reached
to the height of an elbow

and no further: a jill-spring
over dewing meadows at dusk,

her tune a horsehair whicker
cast into long twilight,

to the dye-light; was indigo
purling through water,

a gull-wing sweeping
the fringe from my face –

and her song was a wavelet
accepting the shore's invitation

to land; accepting, and accepting,
one small wave upon another

till the tideline rose in chorus.
This is how we eat away the sand.

ii.

It's a well-known fact
the cello's guts connect
directly to the heart,

its horsehair bow a bonesaw
cutting to the quick
melodic marrow at the core –

except the cello's inner
is a dig, a peaty dark. It needs
an archaeologist's fingers

for its bare revelations. Once,
these rain-sung valleys unearthing
orchestral crackle

from the car radio, I caught
a cello, playing the road
I had come down.

I followed it, driving
out of deep earth, and up
the unmapped passage ahead.

iii.

Chorus
begins behind incisors,
resonates first in the roof

of an unsealed mouth
or mouths, already wonders
what a cupola is for –

containing
the grappled song, perhaps,
or what comes after.

How greedy, how bold
the silence, how complicit
in holding the chords.

Genesis (4)

And Elizabeth, who was born of that rich apportioned soil, begat Mary; and Mary begat Lucy; and Lucy begat Katie.

And Katie took unto herself a husband, and bare fourteen children; and the fifth of these was Arthur, also called Wayne; who was called Bud, which means promises that are yet to be fulfilled.

Statues (Virginia)

i.

They carved their ghosts from rock,
chiselled at the rough superfluous surface
to uncover the good old days at the core:

male and horse-borne, white-featured
in muscular armour, fist balled
at the hilt of his sword, his cloak a billow
defying the absence of wind.

Two blocks from the marketplace
they put him up for exhibition,
laid wreaths at the base of his plinth.

ii.

Our toppled ghosts
we keep in warehouses
on the outskirts of town,

some packed face-down,
others marble-eyeing
the ceiling: stone and metal,

a concentrated weight,
a hidden confederacy of guilt.

iii.

We cannot navigate
by ghosts, though we are still,
so many of us, trying.

Study of My Great Great Great Grandmother, Missouri, 1863

for Mary

The boys are practising war.
In the yard at the edge of the road, sparrows
rejoice at bathing in dust.
Believe God watches all of this:

their jocund rollicking in wheel-ruts, feathered pulses
throwing dirt towards the sky in prayer. Believe
    God watches all of this and cares.

In the yard, your young son's arm
is a repeating rifle, his mouth
a gunshot saying

back –

              back –

as your husband
falls –
       rises –
              only to give him the joy
of falling again. You are out on the edge, on your own
contested land, on the shores of the fighting
they call Civil. Here
war is just another story from the east,

so why shouldn't he shoot
from the pale
unchecked barrel of his fingers? Why not
be jubilant at his father's cruciform drop,
his overblown cry and too-late
clutching of his chest?

And if he makes believe
to turn his aim against the sparrows, then
so what? He can get them all
and not have to stop, to reload.

                              On the porch
your girls are learning their letters,
scratching erratic on the slate.
There's something of guesswork
in their fingers. Even at this age, they understand

space
          is unpredictable –

how their brother
can twitch his fingers over here,

their father
                    collapse in the dirt over there.

So you've told them what you know
about photographs, and distance
caught. And though you have seen no pictures
of the city where your family was born –

rubble, recorded aftermath – you have heard
how they call it
                    shooting.

                              How, fired
                    through the correct aperture, light
can throw person, building, bombarded street
against sensitised plate
with the glass-eyed gaze of the fallen –
how a camera can capture a moment like a torn flag,
and somewhere beyond the lens, a mother
is caught in her grief.

Tonight, you will check
all your children's soft bodies
for parasites –

will thumb the crooked places,
insides of elbows, sacred hollows
at the backs of knees
that still smell, even now, of your milk.

In the burrow of your son's armpit
you will find one, a fattening
tick, gripping
just at the point a man
might brace a rifle butt
against recoil:

                its swelling greed,
its feeding on your firstborn, its giving back
of its own diseases. And you will pinch it
                                full of anger
from his flesh: body, pinned mouth, skin of your son
it fixed to – will drop it
on the embers in the grate, listen hard
for air escaping: squeal like a ghost
fleeing its strict cage of bone.

You have been sewing shirts for soldiers,
dressing them the way their mothers
must have tucked them in at night, the way a nurse
might cover the glass-plate faces of the dead.

How many of your cotton cares
will be buried with their men inside?

How many will burst
like a spray of fresh carnations
on a grave?

Except you know enough
of blood's exit from the body
to know it is never sweet
or perfumed.

You, who have birthed three children,
know the mess made by men
coming into and leaving the world,
the wet brown scud of a soul forcing through.

In the yard, your son begs to be shot,
too keen
                to try his own hand at falling, testing
                        his narrow weight against the air.

He is too far away. Your arms
are too far away. Your husband looks
straight down the barrel of his hand –

                                winks –

        your son is all light, his face
        a gleeful aperture – your husband
        winks, squeezes the slick trigger of air –

and you are running
                        from the porch,
                        from across the yard, and God
        give speed to your legs,
you are running as he falls –

        and your reach
                        is short

                                and you are always

        too far away
                        to catch him.

Two Signs at the Margin of the Interstate

Love Thy Neighbour

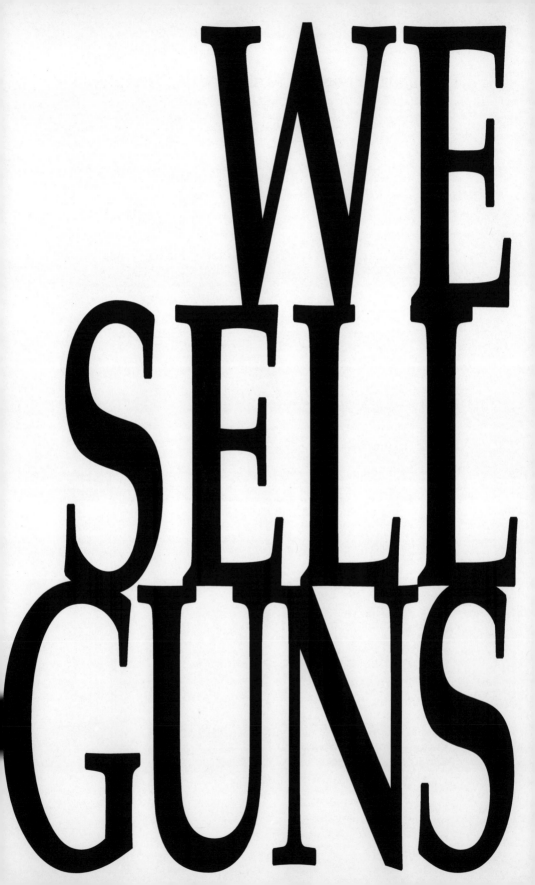

In a Guesthouse in Charlottesville, Virginia, a Telecommunications Engineer Shows Me His Semi-Automatic Handgun

In the coffee-sour kitchen, counter a clean slate
he tilts against, he tells me again
about America's *only ever mass shooting.*

      His wife is a shut trap at the window – and only when
a groundhog ripples the long grass under the trampoline
                  does she say

                                    Cute

        and he says how the dog once lost a groundhog
to the earth, so he tipped in a full can of gasoline
and a match, and his brother
witnessed at the only other exit, loaded
with adrenaline   and shot   and hit
not one, but a family
                a whole fucking family –

and they're here now, running, flanks
quick with terror, each body a sweater flung back, slapped
soft as a prayer on the grass   and still

they keep coming: tens of them, hundreds, a class,
a bar, a whole shopping mall, a nation.

Their heads are silken, smoothed by a trembling
of mothers. Their palisade
is an undergrowth of wrought fingers,
sanctum of hands   each not quite touching the others.

[we apologise: some objects within our collections are being tested for their authenticity]

Portrait of My Whiteness as a Deer

For years I barely saw her, barely felt
her too-sweet breath – her not-tree, not-leaf – loose
as scent between the architectured spruce –
how motherly the branches masked her pelt –

how I moved, she moved, skittish thought, a mirror
with its own intention, tricking the light – as if she,
just by being here, defined the trees,
her tread complicit with the forest floor.

Last night, I dreamed I trapped her, wore her fur,
paraded us down byways, hung my head
on the kitchen wall, where my family gathered, read,
drank tea – and caught – in the flinting heart of deer –

kindled hooves, the smell of cindered bark,
our quick flanks,

              abandoning the treeline as smoke –

Snapshots of My Great Grandmother, Kansas

i.

We share a name by accident: two rivers flowing side by side and never hearing the flood-rush of the other; two pulse-beats running parallel on the monitor of a tracer.

Katie   *Katheros*   *Pure*

She wears her purity like armour, elbow-buffed to reflect her neighbours' squalor. I wear mine as a vice I do not believe in.

ii.

Later, her children will call this farm The Great Place. To her, it is simply a quilt of soil to work, the way she works her knuckles into dough to let it breathe and rise. She seeds it in testing sun, bargains daily for rain. The crop points heavenward, as if the work is God's and not her own. At night, she plants herself in the gaps between her husband's snores, corn stalks creaking in the hot west wind.

iii.

Her knuckles are cow hitches, her fingers tangled rope. She lifts her daughters' petticoats from tub to sky. They flap on the line: the first birds, flaring cotton wings against the wind.

Kneading t-shirts in the chipped bathroom sink of a Kansas motel, I catch ghosts in the mirror: my own hands, my great grandmother's metallic eyes, water pooling like a well.

Streetlamps

after Cavafy

Riding shotgun on a shelterless road to the west,
swerving potholes, dead opossums and racoons,

the sky a lid hinged shut, I can no longer see
whose hands are directing the wheel. At night

the streetlamps are the long-dead women of my family,
spoons of sticky light stacked up in the rear-view mirror.

One appears as a flickering dawn, blue
with unfulfilled desires pooling as skirts at her feet.

One was light-hearted all her life, and now she glows
from within. One stands at a fork in the road and stoops,

reads fortunes in the entrails of roadkill armadillo.
One gets an ache at the back of her neck

whenever it's going to rain. Another is a fatal flame,
draws all the moths to her table, lays on a feast for bats.

I do not want to look at them. I leave them behind.
I bring them with us, the way I lug all journeys.

The road in front of us is dark,
brazen headlights set too bright

but still no sign of a horizon, and no idea
where we might be heading, or to whose destination

or how the little town might look when we arrive –
except there will be a school, a hospital, a bar,

a street with other wanderers parked against the kerb,
a church, its restless audience of graves.

Classification of Foxes

Not wisdom, maybe, like the widespread owl,
nor the eye-bright prescience of weasels –

still, there's cunning in refusing to be named.
Earth of foxes? *Skulk* of foxes? *Leash*?

Earth from the home to which a dog-fox
will return, where a vixen nurses her young.

Skulk from how she will malinger, meaning 'wait
with bad intent': tooth-sharp; hunger-fierce; thief.

The fox, it's said, will grow elusive and difficult
when hunted. *Leash* is only for those kept captive.

My Great Grandmother Crossing the State Border

In that morning before her husband
woke and hitched the horse, she discovered bugs
had crawled under the blanket in the night.
They clung like a second skin to her legs,
a tattoo crawling on her back,
sheathing her arms like gauntlets.
She pinched one between her thumbnails
and it burst the red of river rock –
and though the dawn was sharp with dew
and the fire had all but died, and though
the baby still snuffled and burred in sleep,
she left the wagon and stood
shifted in insects against the rising sun.
Against the red sun she was a city
working at her own making; her skin
commuted and flowed like water.
She plunged her hand into the covering of bugs.
They parted like lips to let her pass.
Plucking at her own skin – thin,
translucent – she peeled it away
like shucking the husks from corn, till her skin
gave way to her flesh and her flesh
stepped aside for her bones.
Her bones she buried in the unmappable prairie,
unmarked, and the prairie gave her back
a body of bugs.
She wore it the rest of her life.
On nights her husband lay beside her,
they tingled and swarmed to his touch,
became a nest of desire. When he hit her,
tiny mouths bit and scratched at his fists.
Later, her children were born with insect hearts;
they dispersed and gathered like a colony.
The day she died, her body
scattered. The bed, rippling in the lamplight,
smelled of her life: of leaf mould and hunger.

Earthrise, 1968

The year has barely begun to grip
before her ghost
drops through, pitches into the unexcavated sky,

before her narrow death-wheeze becomes
a dusty unlit road
approaching the horizon –

and down it Martin Luther King is always
still alive, drawing breath as my great grandmother
lets slip her last – before the raised

black fists of Smith and Carlos punch through
the star-spangled anthem like conductors
calling lightning from the clouds –

and a thousand miles away and still
unlit, Apollo 8 is caught in the act
of being made –

though she has begun
her long yearning towards the launchpad,
towards the moon's occipital bone,

towards home
rising
blue and spotlit from the night, looking

for all the world
like a live wire, humming
at the epicentre of the dark,

a lustrous unspent coin.

Genesis (5)

And Bud sought out war to the east, and there did take for himself a wife, Dorothy, daughter of Jane, called Jennie.

And thus he did return to the west, and Dorothy with her daughter after; and there she begat a second daughter, called Val.

My Grandmother and the Coyote

It's true she first met him in the park,
pushing her niece in the coach-built pram,
him yapping some quip about babes.
He had breezed across the ocean on the weather –
all wisecracks and cheap
jackal laugh, incisors lipped.

And it's true she first met him at a dance
where girls surged in their thin
print dresses, and in the band
the Home Guard blew up a storm,
my grandparents face-to-face shores
of the Atlantic. They say coyotes
are supposed to mate for life.

And it's true she was a sensible girl
but he was good-looking and American,
song dog with harmonics in his gait. He led her
down the narrow corridors of scales
where every slick note was a door.

And it's true they first met
on the threshold of the Royal Ordnance Factory,
her bound for her break, him
loping down the byway with the troops,
that he called the dogged convoy to a stop,
his cry a steam train shrieking on the tracks.

The road was hidden from view
but it's true he was a harbinger of ending
and of birth, that his fur
furrowed grey and fulvous, and he bristled
at changes in the wind.

In their honeymoon London hotel, his breath
settled as meat. His eyes were lit and liquid yolks
and she believed she was part of his pack.

He curled and lengthened beside her on the mattress,
his body the weight of a filled suitcase.

[we apologise: many doors are kept closed to maintain the correct conditions]

My Grandmother Marries a G.I.

on the sideboard was a box we were never allowed to open   the base
made a dust-window on the wood   lid a cold sky fretted with crows
and on days we lolled by the telly or sprawled puzzles on the laminate   we
thought we heard something inside it   crying like an old gate
its sides seemed thin as the room   but sometimes they were the grey walls
of the town   smut-clogged   pocked with shrapnel   or else
were metal and red brick   the cellophane factory birthing its sulphuric
pong   and at its base the heavy threat of footfall on a road   we
peeked around the back   to the crack between box and living room wall
     and the side turned away was the church   studded door   beetle-
black nave   dark-stone aisle once walked by all the women in my family
     at its finish always a man   the box had a hinge made from hands
     from clasped knuckles   forbidden as unlit streets where the Luftwaffe
skimmed overhead like an outbreath   or the thistle-choked towpath by
Newtown Lock   there was always a catch   keyless metal loop
     tight as cleat hitches mooring the boats to the docks   let us
open it now   fold back those long-dead afternoons with corvids
exploiting the updraft   military slate roofs   steeple questioning the sky
          lean closer   let us look inside

Home

you send your parents back before the ship casts off

they will make it   but later snow
will bawl about the house you used to share
frost spit obscenities through the gaps
and you will worry they might run out of fuel

/

and later when the man at the immigration desk
speaks   it is almost the voice of your husband

but isn't   and when he asks your family name
he no longer means the one you were born to

/

and later   when you give up your seat
to the man on the bus   he will tell you
    this is not allowed in this country
not for a white woman   not for a black man

and later your friend   your kindest
wife-of-a-German friend   will be barred
by your husband from the house

and later   a neighbour will leave you
sacks of potatoes on the stoop   will say
she ordered the extra by mistake

/

come home
says the wind begging you back to the Atlantic

home
says the squirming daughter at your breast

but the Manifest of Alien Passengers is the size
of a Bible   and the name on the page says

you are already home   come in   now keep walking

On Telling My Grandmother How the MS John Ericsson Was Scrapped in Bilbao, Spain, in 1965

But the ship, you tell me, burned in New York Harbour.

The ship was a metal womb. No, the ship was a woman, lumbering through squalls, rough as guts and harder than bone, her belly filled with children. She birthed you and your daughter onto a baleful shore, and years later, burned in the harbour.

The ship, you insist, gave in to engine failure, or a cigarette tip, or any other searing hurt that sets a life ablaze – unlocked her rivets and let her joints reach wide, unfolding herself on the quayside like a paper boat. The deckhands were thumb-smears and she swallowed them whole.

The ship could not be saved, not by all the waters of the Atlantic. She burned, white-hot and credible as your American Dream. She blazed for days, and all the women of my family tossed their own truths on, to fuel or quench her, nobody could say. Menfolk told how she screamed with burning, a sound metallic and loud as her own body, but the women said no – this is what rapture sounds like.

The ship was magnificent in her ending. Her procreating pillar of smoke could be seen across three states and seven intervening decades.

You tell it like this: the ship disassembled herself into the sea, the crowds dispersed and water lapped at the monochrome docks, and that was the end of that. I say, if only we could go back, raise her from the waves, still grandiose with flame – if only we were close enough to burn –

Fox in Snow

I was twelve the winter her bold red body slunk out of the trees
to cross the unbroached white. In the centre of the lawn, she stopped,
sniffed, raised a questioning paw, then printed her steady line

across the waiting snow. The camera was in the desk drawer
where it always was, new film locked in plastic canisters like bullets –
so we made no record of the fox. Years later when I ask my mum

she can't remember. Isn't sure. It's taken half my life and more
to beg this fox onto the page. No ticking clock. No *sudden sharp hot stink*.
Even now she shifts letters, noses her own path through the text.

Was it winter? Had it snowed? Did the fox burn red, her coat a spill
of fire, a passing shiver? No spoor left lingering on leaves,
no drag, no echoing bark. So little left to prove her, one way or the other.

Bridal

Stalled in tissue paper:
my grandmother's rein of hair

still taut at the gates
for her long furlongs,

for seventy years
untethered in the drawer

The Wagon

after Vasko Popa

Someone be the wagon.
Someone be the horse.
Everyone else be the road.

The wagon must hitch herself
to the horse, must let herself be
pulled by the horse
and let the road furrow under her.

The horse must tug till the ring
clangs at his bit
and the wagon is pulled after.

If the wagon baulks, the horse
kicks her loose, then gets to raise
a new wagon
from the ones who are being the road.

This is how the game is won:
the first wagon becomes the sound of wheels
and keeps on playing alone.

Portrait of My Grandma, Listening

the stones   mouths full with old rain
were cantillating in the crumbled nave

can't you hear   you said   *they're singing*
plainchant   but I was in my buggy asleep
and my mother in her reversible mac
said   *nobody's singing mum*

so   as if the ruin had a centrefold
and this was it   you stood
where you could choose to read
forwards or back   and listened

later   I will tell a child who is not
my daughter   why the abbey is so quiet
because the king was longing
for another woman   and a son

later I will listen to the lost air   its single melody
see how lifting off the roof lets the light rush in

Nimbus

after Berndnaut Smilde

Some days, my grandma is a cloud –
her face a god-ray and the sheets
blue-white as insides of wrists.
Some days, she needs only air
to hold her aloft from the bed
in the big dark room. There must be
a moon somewhere, because
my grandma is a swatch of snow.

In the fourth episode this morning
about a man who still talks
to his partner's ghost, furniture
is floating of its own accord –
though really this is done with electricity
and magnets. Some days, my grandma
has her own current inside her

and maybe this is how I can stand
in the space beneath her, scratch
the plastic floor with my shoes
where she casts no shadow,
where she has lightning pent
in her breast. Some days, she is
heavy as rain. Her body is a flood
making all roads out impassable.

After my grandma dies

I hear foxes in the night outside her flat:
mother tilting wharf-like towards the still water;
two scrappy calamitous cubs, racing the length of the dock.

All along the converted warehouses, curtains twitch
like noses catching scent – to let the lamplight in,
to watch (without being watched) the cubs' abandon:

how they stalk with held breath – or roll in grass
the council have forgotten to strim – or thunder like dogs,
all bark and yip and goading their mother to look.

Next morning over the phone, I'll describe this for my mum.
Later, my aunt will tell me they make their home
on the mump at the back of the grain store – the one building

to hold to its original purpose – though even that, she'll say,
will soon move out of town. Everything passes. The bark
of the no-nonsense vixen. Her brash and vulnerable daughters.

Genesis (6)

And Val begat a daughter, called Katie, which means pure, because she wished purity upon her; and so began her daughter to call up the names of the women; and her daughter went out from the continent of birth.

The Call

Soon after I moved out, my mother
woke in the dark to a fox calling her name –
a gruff harsh bark like a smoker's cough,
recognition so sharp it punctured the night.
She lay for almost an hour as it summoned her.
Once or twice, she almost woke my dad,
but women in our family have always heard
what no one else can hear, and this was not his fox.
She felt the tug of it like rope, as if it had
gnawed into her and clamped its snarl
around her insides, as if her death was small
and russet coloured. Come to think of it,
she had always known her life would end in fox:
the velvet pad of paws, the darkness, the solitary
torch of a tail. She came from earth women,
strong as forests, who worked metal and soil
with their hands, and like all earth women
she was burrow bound. She lay in eiderdown
and waited for her body to respond.

'Write plainly, with unfading ink – this is a permanent record'

Certificate of Death
Lucy Jane Riggs, 1910

Lanterns, Kansas, 1997

The dark was close enough to touch
when we took jam jars from the shelf
to trap the lightning bugs

and hung them from the tree – a festoon
blinking in the blue evening.

I don't remember any thought
of setting them free. How pale

our hands were then, how small.
They fluttered in the glitter-light like moths.
We sat all night beneath the swaying glass.

White Woman Tears

Today on Twitter, a white woman,
called *racist* for pushing to be published
in a journal that platforms women of colour,

has posted her response: crying
rudeness, crying *deep hurt*, crying *victim*.
And no, I have never done anything like this, but

I know how culpability can choke
like brine in the gullet, the gut's reaction
always to hawk it back up, spit it out.

And by *never*, ~~I mean maybe, I can't remember~~
~~I mean it's a privilege to be able to forget~~
~~I mean as a woman, as a white woman, maybe once~~

I mean when I learned I come from slaveowners
my first response was shame, my second response
to write a poem about that shame

~~because there's a theory that ink is a revolt~~
~~against the whiteness of the page~~
~~but also that writing in English means~~

~~a poem will always speak with the tongue~~
~~of oppression~~ I mean sometimes tears
are made of words instead of brine

~~though by *words*, I mean tough-to-swallow~~
~~I mean not-all-words I mean~~ sometimes words
are made of brine instead of water

[we apologise: some items from our weapons display are currently being exhibited abroad]

I was born in the morning

slithered out of the cut in my mother,
a thing no bigger than a bacon rind

and squalling. *There was something
of the fox about you*, she said later,

a cub lifted too soon from the den.
She watched my birth

in the sheet-metal ceiling,
her other self a storm-cloud

brewing at dusk, a small fire
far too far from the beach.

Then my mother unfurled her body.
Her arms were scrubbed tough

and she caught me. All through my life
she has rocked my reflection

as I head for the uncharted deep.

Fish

Slip of metal, little flicker I netted
from the beck at the bottom of the village,

how you suspended yourself, silent
in your margarine tub world. How I

watched for your rapid shivers, mercury
broken from the bulb, the liquid shift,

how you would rise till your spine
feathered the surface, then drop,

go still, wait,
how once I tried to time

my breath to your stillness
but had to let go. How I would

blink, then think I'd missed
your quick arabesques. Little fish

how you waited
till my back was turned, to fling yourself

out into the world, a new coin tumbling,
till the dark mouth of the plughole

took you in. O how I picture you
still, my sequinned escapologist,

flickering on through the pipes, to where
the depth of a river lies calling.

at a reading, a white woman asks what good it does to be always harping on about the past

harp like *hope* – isn't that what a harp is? horsehair/catgut/string
anticipating touch, always singing of past holdings

harp like *harpy* – how a voice can grow claws, can be bred
to never let go, wings beating repeated downdraft

and speaking of beating – harp like *heart* – though don't fugues suggest
we only notice rhythm when it changes? and besides

harp is an old word, roots uncertain –
harfe / harpa / hearpe – though the dictionary says

it's probably from *skreb* – a reconstructed word, only invented
for bridging a gap – meaning *to shrink / to touch / to attack*

An Unstoppable Force Meets an Immovable Object

At the roof of the Rockies is the watershed
of America, the great divide,

where you can stand astride
the continental split, can gob your spit

(each gene-coded cell of it) one hawk to east
then west – then watch as each

begins its slow
globular journey towards opposing waters:

Pacific with her quarrel of fire,
Atlantic, wrecker of ships.

And this is how a body can be pulled
in two directions: my mother,

newborn and uprooted to a hospital crib,
parents' marriage gone to tectonic drift

and both her grandmothers warm
colliding fronts from either side.

They say these mountains were a man
once, who asked to go on forever

and was granted. A strong desire
phrased badly – though I too have wished

to be landscape in a foreign age,
to be cradled by wrangling oceans,

let trees take root in my bones,
to let them drink from deep on either side –

let new leaves whisper *this is not enough* –
unrest give voice to the wind –

Portrait of a White Enamel Jug, 1874

for Lucy, my great great grandmother

It's late afternoon and the sun is the colour of biscuits.
It slides through the panes at a furtive angle,
slender thief sidling into the house.
There's a cluster of vetch in the jug
at the back of the sink. It droops
like old women coughing, already
smells of dust and dying summers.
A field away, James and the horses
lag against the uphill pull. In just a few weeks
the grasshoppers will bear down
like a rasping army from the north
and all the year's corn will be undone.
In the bottom of the frame,
the tiny hand of a child who will one day
pull my great grandmother from her body
reaches up to tug the purple blooms.

Acknowledgements and Thanks

Italicised lines in 'Portrait of My Great Great Great Great Great Great Great Grandmother as Emily Shelby in *Uncle Tom's Cabin*' are taken from *Uncle Tom's Cabin* by Harriet Beecher Stowe.

'And in the sequel' references Disney's *Frozen 2*, alongside a digitisation project run by New York Botanical Gardens, and is for Sarah Dutton, who pushed for repatriation of the remains mentioned in the poem.

'Fox in Snow' references images from 'The Thought Fox' by Ted Hughes.

Thank you to Jane Commane and Angela Hicken at Nine Arches, and to my agent Lucy Luck at Conville & Walsh. Thank you also to Malika Booker, whose mentorship during the editing process was invaluable.

In 2018, I received a DYCP grant from Arts Council England, to support travel to the US to research and write the collection, for which I am enormously grateful. Thank you also to New Writing North for a 2021 Northern Writers' Debut Award to support me to edit the book, and to Cumbria Community Foundation's Cultural Fund for a grant to attend an Arvon Course.

I would also like to thank everyone involved in the following residencies, where many poems in the book were written and edited: MacDowell; Wordsworth Grasmere; Hawthornden Castle; Gladstone's Library; Heinrich Böll Cottage (funded by Mayo County Council and Arts Council of Ireland); The Writers' House of Georgia (enabled by Desperate Literature and the de Groot Foundation); and Passa Porta (enabled by The National Centre for Writing and the Flemish Literature Fund). Thank you also to the Milstein Division of United States History, Local History & Genealogy at New York Public Library, to Cane Ridge Meeting House, KY, to Sarah Davy and Northern Writers' Studio – and to Arvon, Kendal Poetry Festival, Kim Moore, Pascale Petit, Ann and Peter Sansom, and George Szirtes for the workshops where some of these poems began life.

Thanks to the following publications where some of these poems first appeared: *Magma, Mslexia, Palette Poetry,* and *Under the Radar.* Poems from the collection also won the Jane Martin Prize, the Palette Poetry Prize, and the Prole Laureate Prize; were shortlisted or placed in the Bridport Prize, the *Magma* Editors' Prize, the Manchester Poetry Prize, the *Mslexia* Poetry Prize, the Oxford Brookes Poetry Competition, and the University of Canberra Vice Chancellor's International Poetry Competition; and were commended in the *Magma* Editors' Prize, the Newcastle Poetry Competition, the Otley Poetry Prize, and the Verve Poetry Competition. 'Fish' and 'I was born in the morning' were first published in my chapbook, *Assembly Instructions* (Southword, 2019).

Thank you to all those who have read these poems in earlier drafts: members of Brewery Poets, Dove Cottage Poets, and Poety Club; fellow writers and artists at Hawthornden and MacDowell; Polly Atkin, Elizabeth Mann and Jessi Rich. And finally, thank you to Loren, and to my family, for your continued inspiration and support.